The Wisdom of Being
and Guide to Becoming

Perfectly

Imperfect

Shelley Meaney

The Wisdom of Being and Guide to Becoming
PERFECTLY IMPERFECT
Shelley Meaney

ISBN

978-0-6152-0561-8

1.

Terra Celeste Productions
4144 San Martin Way
Santa Barbara CA 93110
USA
shelley@shelleysbellys.com

For Stacy Stephanie and Mom.

*I wouldn't be who I am today
without your loving encouragement
...even when I wore a getup.*

Perfectly Imperfect

CONTENTS

PREFACE

JUST ASK
2
LIVE DANGEROUSLY
4
SPEAK YOUR TRUTH
6
STARDUST
8
THE FORCE
10
FLOW
12
HELP YOURSELF
14
I'M NOT PERFECT
16
TRUE LOVE
18
TAKE OUT THE TRASH
20
MY MOST EMBARRASSING MOMENT
22
FORCED TO CHANGE
24
RIGHT WHERE I BELONG
26
GRATITUDE IN THE FITTING ROOM
28

EMBRACING THE SUCK

30

IN DEEP

32

LUST FOR LIFE

34

GO THERE

36

FULL

38

VACATION

40

PRESENCE

42

LOUD AND CLEAR

44

SERENITY IN THE CHAOS

46

THERE IS NO RIGHT WAY

48

CONFIRMATION

50

BREATHE IN JOY

52

TEACHERS

54

YOU CAN'T HATE YOURSELF

56

HOW TO MAKE IT ALL FUN

58

THE EVOLUTION OF DOUBT

60

SECRET

64

LOVE
66
YOU MAY NOT BELIEVE THIS
68
TRANSFORMATION
70
PRESENTS
72
DOING YOUR BEST
74
GIFTS
76
LIVING LIKE THERE'S NO TOMORROW
78
LET DEATH BE A REMINDER
82
IT'S ONLY CALLED DROWNING
84
WANT TO BET?
86
PERFECTLY IMPERFECT
88
MATURITY MEANS LETTING GO
90
YOU ONLY LIVE ONCE
92
DISCOMFORT SERVES A PURPOSE
94
NOT QUITE WHAT YOU HAD IN MIND
96
MEMOIRS OF A WICKED STEPMOTHER
98
THE BEST GIFTS
100

DESTINY
102
CHANGED
106
IN THE AIR
108
METAPHOR
110
FAMILY DISCOUNT
112
WHAT'S THE WORST THAT COULD HAPPEN?
116
A NEW SET OF BOOBS
120
NOTHING IS EVER LOST
122
BE AN AMATEUR
124
LIGHTEN YOUR HEART
126

PREFACE

Always a seeker of the depths in people, truth and mysteries of the universe, I have studied many fields. When I was ten, I wanted to be an astronaut and began my studies in astronomy. When I was fifteen, I wanted to be a writer and began to devour books and keep a journal. When I was twenty, I wanted to be a physician and studied the human body in health and disease and eventually found myself working in pharmaceutical sales. In my thirties, I fell in love with gemstones, the poetry of geology and the earth's natural history. I have always marveled at the human experience and how some people thrive in joy while others simply exist and still others seem to struggle in their every day experiences.

My perspective frequently includes commonalities and connections that may not be obvious to others.

Having experienced and lived with depression in the insidious form that makes you think that it is "normal" and then in a concentrated from after the birth of my children, that finally led me to diagnosis and treatment, I have come to believe that each and every person on the planet has the potential to live a blissful life. What I have written here is my own personal experience and observations toward obtaining this goal. Here I expose myself for scrutiny so that you may share in my perspective, which is that you do not have to be perfect to be *perfect*.

JUST ASK

As an experiment, might I suggest simply asking for that which you deeply desire? Or perhaps stating with confidence that it is desired and that you are willing to work for it and that you will appreciate it when you have it. Go ahead. Try it. I will too. "I want to walk on the moon." I do. I expect that someday, I will. How I will finance my private journey is not important, only that I ask and move consciously toward my goal. As of today, at the very least, my passport is valid.

LIVE DANGEROUSLY

Live dangerously. Live foolishly. Live embarrassingly. Live sillily. Live sadly. Live joyfully. Fear not the impact you will have by being you. Part the waters. Cause a wave. Dare to be stared at. Inspire thought and courage. When you go to high tea in Beverly Hills, wear a hat and gloves. Sip your tea as if you were a princess or a movie star. When traveling to Alaska in the winter, wear your huge moon boots on the plane, let them take up the entire under-seat space in front of you. Laugh at yourself. Embody the experience. Embarrass your friends and family. Live.

SPEAK YOUR TRUTH

I have a conscious memory of shutting myself up. Sometime in my childhood, during developmental years, I was way wrong and it made a deep impression. It is so humiliating to speak up and be wrong.

Sometimes, the lesson learned isn't "to keep learning until you get it right", but to shut off your voice, your opinion and your truth so you never have to subject yourself to that humiliation again. Now, as an adult, I have broken through that self silencing by realizing you can't actually die from embarrassment, and have come to realize that being "wrong" is as profound and important as being "right".

The earthly experience is a pendulous one, swinging from one extreme to the other so that all sides of an experience or a feeling may be appreciated. This is why compassion is such an important tool. To judge others, and especially oneself, is to risk limiting the profound physical and emotional experiences to be had in life. Today, I encourage you, I actually dare you, to speak what is on your mind, let those thoughts be heard. See what happens when you do.

STARDUST

Did you know that YOU are made of stardust? You are, and so is everything else on this planet. What we know about stars is that first generation stars begin with elemental hydrogen (one proton, one electron) and fuse the atoms together to form the slightly heavier element, helium. The amazing energy that comes from this fusion is what the sun and other stars emit. When all the hydrogen is consumed, the helium atoms start fusing, into lithium. These are pretty simple elements and a first generation star runs out of fuel before any heavy elements, like metals, are created. The heaviest elements, like iron and lead are created when a star explodes, or goes "supernova". So, we know that our star is a second or possibly a third generation star and that we, and everything on this planet has been formed out of the dust of that mega-explosion.

Just imagine all the wonderful things that occurred before this very second. All the steps the universe has taken to bring us all here to this point in time. Doesn't it put a smile on your face? You are a part of all of it. The Universe is you. You are the Universe.

THE FORCE

I'm not really big on blind faith. I generally need to know how, why, when, all the way back to the earliest, most elemental point of something. I believe this is why I am so enthralled by physics, chemistry, geology, evolution, astronomy, anthropology and medicine. I need to know how the universe began, and everything after that. In detail. The more I learn about it all, the more I am romanced by this type of information.

When I started buying rocks and gems eight years ago, it was natural for me to not just take the beauty of the stones at face value. I learned by investigation that gemstones affect living things. They are used as healing tools by themselves worn close to the body, used within a given space or area for cleansing energy or other purposes, in elixirs and salves for health and healing. My natural process has brought me to the point of investigating how and why gemstones affect people.

A little back story: ever since I was a kid, seeing *Star Wars, The Empire Strikes Back* for the first time (This is the one where Yoda explains to Luke what The Force is), the concept of The Force as an energy that permeates all things, that connects and binds us all with the universe, has rung true to me.

What does The Force have to do with gemstones? Gemstones are crystals. Crystals are solid forms of matter in their most organized, stable state. They form lattice structures with repeating patterns and, like all things, they vibrate in this organized state. All atoms vibrate. Even the most solid form you can imagine is vibrating. An electron "cloud" surrounds the nucleus of every atom. We can only imagine the general whereabouts of an electron at any given

10

moment, that's how much it moves. If we are all made up of these energetic atoms and we are all connected by the atoms in the air we exist in, and some things vibrate in a more harmonized way, (and, like adding hot water to cold water makes warm water) then gemstones provide a more orderly vibration to help neutralizes a more chaotic vibration.

Gemstones affect our bodies, our emotions, and our spiritual energies, leaving us in a more positive and healthy state. I have had countless experiences with my stones and wear a daily arrangement based on what I intuitively am drawn to as needing. I have a Russian Amazonite pendant that I wore almost every day last year. It made me feel calmer, more resolute, inspired and less fearful.

Trusting your intuition when it comes to gemstones is an effective way to choose what you need. I find myself attracted to certain colors or stones when I get dressed for the day or am creating a piece for someone. When you learn to listen to your self by trusting your feelings, you gain access to your intuition and strengthen your connection to the energy all around you.

FLOW

I would describe myself as easy going. I think that's part of the secret of my success as a parent. My house is chaotic and messy. My kids are loud and lively. My life is fast and furious and I LOVE IT! When I was little, growing up in Manhattan Beach, spending my summers playing in the ocean waves, I learned that when you get caught in a big one it's better if you don't struggle. Relax. Be like laundry in the washing machine. If you are this way, when you get pulled under and tossed around in the waves, you never seem to run out of air in your lungs and the wave eventually passes. When it's over, you just stand up, pull your bikini back on, smile and say whoa, that was awesome!!!

Go with the flow. Don't fight, struggle, fear or tighten. Relax, ride, enjoy the foamy green water and worry not. You are tougher than you think.

HELP YOURSELF

One of the secrets to the joyous life I have discovered for myself is passing it on. You want joy? Pass it on. You want love? Pass it on. You want recognition? Pass it on. Give it away to get it. Pass it on to make it flow.

More than half of the jewelry I make is given away. Sometimes I create an unexpected surprise and just send something off. The joy I get from reaching out and shaking up someone's day is so enlivening for me. I get a spark of desire to do something for someone else and it instantly fires me up with creative energy, drive, inspiration and happiness.

This works in relationships too. You want an apology? Say you're sorry. You want a hug? Give one. You want acknowledgment? Give it. You want to have a meaningful friendship? Be a true friend. You want generosity? Give give give. The secret is to risk by being the first one to act. Try it. It may inspire those you encounter to be less selfish, less superficial, less angry, less self-centered, less rude, more friendly, more open, more fun, more generous, more loving, more apologetic, more attentive and of course, more happy.

I'M NOT PERFECT

What I do with gemstones is risky. I make a promise. I take a leap. I go out on a limb. Can I really do this? Am I qualified? Can people really trust me?

The loudest voice inside of me says YES!!!! That voice says,

"you are a spiritual being on a human journey. You are not meant to be perfect all the time. Sometimes you will be wrong, you will make mistakes, you will say, 'I'm sorry'. But what you are doing is from your heart. It is not forced; it flows. You come from love and you feel love when you work. You infuse your love into every piece you make. There is nothing but good in this."

So, intuitively, I know that I am capable, trustworthy and engaging in my life's work.

The trigger of self scrutiny happened when someone I respect, who has been working with stones longer than I have, held up a mirror to me and questioned my process and my use of gemstones for therapeutic purposes. The small amount of self-doubt in me, that will probably always lurk in every healthy practitioner, showed itself and hit a nerve, causing a flood of tears. If I were counseling someone in the exact situation, I would tell him or her, "Keep going. It's O.K. to risk making mistakes; this is how you learn things. Trust your gut, your intuition. When people question your abilities or your process, thank them and listen. Good leaders are not gods. Those who never admit their mistakes or their shortcomings are not true leaders or practitioners." And because I can be gentle and nurturing with others, I will try to be gentle and nurturing with myself and I will take my own good advice, which is to risk making mistakes and when you do, call it *learning*. Never stop learning. Do what you love no matter how you are received.

TRUE LOVE

I am both a daughter and a mother and what I can tell you is that the bond between child and parent represents the first true love. As a child I remember feeling such a deep feeling of love for my mother, the thought of losing her made me ache and cry with pain.

As I grew, this desperate fear subsided and I was able to appreciate the entertainment value of our relationship. Anyone who knows my mother will agree that she is an incredible woman: funny, smart, creative, generous and loving. I think I love the fact that she has always been a fun and amusing companion most. We have amazing discussions, laughing often.

My mother writes poetry. It flows through her. She can't help herself. She practically speaks in prose. She never ceases to amuse me. A couple of years ago she fell backwards from a standing position down a short flight of concrete stairs. She spent her 57th birthday in the ICU and could have easily died from the intracranial bleeding and swelling. Not only did she pull through, she wrote the most amazing poem about the experience. Anyone who can take this situation, write about it, and in the telling, make you laugh and smile is someone extraordinary. Yeah. My mom really is amazing. And I know it. I don't take our relationship for granted. She was my first, truest and deepest love.

I am so grateful to have had my heart stretched with love to the size that it is. It now swells so big with love for my kids, my husband, family and friends that I think the energy of it could literally wrap around the planet twice, like a big, huge hug.

TAKE OUT THE TRASH

By reaching out and saying what we need, we are able to activate the universe into delivering. So often I am bothered by something, or feel despondent, alone or in pain, and my salvation comes when I talk it out. It's like taking out the trash. After I've done it, really emptied all the worries, fears and issues honestly, I feel relief, and I can go on. I am lucky. I have two sisters, a mother and friends whom I employ regularly as my heart's trash collectors. They are supportive, non judgmental and loving, no matter what. I am also skilled at reciprocating the favor, to anyone who needs me. I know how powerful it can be to unload the negativity and resentment, the fear and the worry from your heart.

The truth is, that even if your outlet is a journal or a pet, a trustworthy stranger or your guardian angel, you are not alone and these burdens need not be yours to bear. Let the universe help with your load and trust that you are heard, seen and loved. And just remember that we are all made from the same stardust. Even in our solitude, we will always be connected, supported, nurtured and loved.

MY MOST EMBARRASSING MOMENT

I am looking at a picture of myself. I am wearing a hat and gloves for Tea. It was December 2005. My sisters and I made reservations at some chichi hotel in Beverly Hills to surprise our mother for her 59th birthday by taking her and all of our female children to High Tea.

I made Mom a card and insisted that we all don hats and gloves for this special occasion. My sisters thought this was a VERY BAD idea. They said, "we wouldn't be caught dead in vintage hats and gloves- no way- absolutely not." Mom said she would do it, as I knew she would. She is always game for adding a little theatrical spice to her experiences. So, being the defiant woman, and little sister that I am, I tucked a choice hat and pair of gloves from Mom's extensive vintage dress-up collection into my handbag and off we went to tea. After our order was taken, I pulled my accessories out and put them on.

"You are NOT wearing that!!" my sister Stephanie said, and yet, her amusement was evident, as it always is when she tells me that I have on a "nice getup". I love this response so much that I often don creative "getups" just for her.

My secret? I'm beyond mortification. I have been in more humiliating, embarrassing situations than I can count. I haven't died yet. For example, eighth grade, I forgot to zip my fly after fourth period P.E. on the day that all my respectable panties were dirty and I was forced to wear the ones with the kids bowling in hot pink graphics. As I sat innocently on the grass eating my lunch, Peter Gently, a cute and very popular boy, stood over me and said, "nice underwear" with a sneer.

Then there was the time in 11th grade when I walked very quickly down the crowded hall, to the bathroom only to find a baseball sized spot of blood on the back of my white Norma Kamali skirt.

I've gone down the ski slopes in the "bucket", the body-length toboggan they strap you into to get you safely off the slopes, after doing my impersonation of a human snow ball, sang solo and slightly off key at my sister's wedding, been seen in multitudes of creative but not necessarily fashionable "get ups", called people by the wrong name, had my slip show, have forgotten to wear a slip, had lipstick on my teeth, had my breast exposed or my skirt pulled down by a tantrumming toddler, I have even called attention to my, large, wide ass by dancing to the song "I Like Big Butts" for our family talent show, and much, much more.

I am immune to embarrassment. I actually like the spice it gives to my life and others' by taking the seriousness out and putting humility and humor in. So, next time you have an embarrassing moment or have the opportunity to dress up, I would like to encourage you to stand out instead of blending in. Take the risk of embarrassing yourself. It won't kill you, it will remind you that you are human and part of being truly human is making "mistakes" and feeling silly. You can bet that you will never be alone, so you might as well enjoy it.

As for my MOST embarrassing moment? I don't think I've experienced it just yet. It may just be sharing this book with you.

23

FORCED TO CHANGE

Two years ago, I lost my position as a pharmaceutical representative with Merck. I had worked for Merck for nine years and being the loyal, patient person that I am, probably never would have left. A realignment of the sales force left me without my job but allowed me to retain my dignity and gradually, through the generosity of severance pay, learn how to cope as a "kept woman". I used to juggle like nobody's business. My marriage, role as a mother, stepmother, hardworking member of a team, educated, intelligent, informed face in front of physicians, and of course, I had my own creative needs.

Thinking back on it now, I don't know how I did it. I am now a full time mother, stepmother, wife, writer, photographer, jewelry designer and creator, etc. I also keep the house running, the bills paid, the oil changed in the car, the animals fed, work in the classroom, try to exercise regularly, maintain friendships not to mention the almost daily trips to all the different grocery stores. I know you know what I am talking about because your life is most likely very similar to mine. Do you find yourself with a half an hour and no commitments and ask yourself, "What can I get done in this small window of time?" Do you weigh the pros and cons of not picking up the toys that litter the living room floor and what you could do for yourself during the time it would take for you to vacuum the scuzzy carpet? I do. I figure that eventually, the kids will grow up and retreat to the confines of their rooms and, in time, they will move away.

My husband and I will have a zen sanctuary with bubbling fountains in our gardens and sleek, yet comfortable, modern furniture in our living areas that we will be proud to share with friends. Yes, we will have it all. Abundance, prosperity, personal achievements to be proud of, time to relax and enjoy the quiet.

Since losing my job I have realized I am loyal and persistent and sometimes have to be forced into change. My perspective has revealed that unexpected change brings forth unexpected outcomes and seeing the change as an opportunity makes the future a lot more exciting. I have also realized that when given a tad bit more time to work with, I am not inclined to spend it on keeping a house clean. Cleanliness at this stage of life just seems like a waste of time to me.

RIGHT WHERE I BELONG

Have you ever heard of "divine timing"? It's the reason you sometimes feel like you don't fit in or things just aren't going the way you want them to, or why you haven't gotten "there" yet, assuming you know where it is you want to be. Divine timing, I was reminded yesterday, as I pulled it from my angel oracle deck, means that certain things have to happen in order for you to get where you need to be.

Haven't you ever completed something and seen that the precarious situations that seemed so wrong were actually essential to the achievement of that final outcome? O.K., So right at this very moment, I am here to remind you that you are right where you need to be. Let your heart rest easy and worry not. Hold yourself in gratitude for all the hardships that have brought you to this point and remember to enjoy the journey. It won't last forever and the timing is not only perfect, it's *divine*.

GRATITUDE IN THE FITTING ROOM

I was trying on the new "miracle suit" one-piece bathing suit at Nordstrom the other day. I wanted to see if I really did look ten pounds lighter in ten seconds. Here's what I saw. If I had been gazing not at myself but on some other woman in the black cross over one piece, I would have thought, *she looks nice, elegant, sleek, handsome, not a waif, but a woman, full and lovely.*

What I thought of myself was... I am wide, very wide from behind, my skin is lumpy, dimpled and discolored with bruises and spider veins, and where did my real body go? You know what I'm talking about. The body that was free and easy in a bikini. The body I used to self-consciously wrap a towel around for the trip from my beach blanket to the water. Where is my real body?

Why is this memory of my former self the model for comparison? I haven't looked like that in many years. I am thirty-nine now, still comparably young and younger than I will ever be. My body still allows me to be comfortably mobile, to wrestle my children into submission, to travel, to enjoy things like food and wine, flowers and stars. My body can hear music and still dance to it. My body can make jewelry and write this essay.

I realize that my body is beautiful. It is *my* gift and absolutely deserves to be cherished, even in its lumpy, puckered, blotchy form.

EMBRACING THE SUCK

Sometimes the key to gratitude is walking into discomfort. I can remember vividly the summer after college graduation when I spent two months in Ecuador to participate in medical research with two of my favorite college professors and another student who became my good friend.

Those sixty days were long, hot, dirty, and lonely in addition to being influential and beneficial for character building. We were stuck a lot in gooey, sticky, boot-sucking mud on long trails that led to houses with no toilets, outhouses or running water. No gas for fire, no dry wood for cooking, and of course, no electricity. This was the trip that started in a cheap hotel in Quito, where Dr. Rudy's backpack (with all of his money, eyeglasses, radio and other important things) was stolen on the first day, and prostitutes had the bed in the next room squeaking all night. This trip also started with a drive in a cab through a cloud of smoke that burned my eyes and nose and turned out to be tear gas from a riot to protest the escalation of the price of fuel.

When the sixty days were over, and I was home again, my heart swelled with gratitude for the modern conveniences which were really luxuries. A flushing toilet, warm water, a gas stove that you could just cook on, clean water that you could just drink, paved roads. And my heart swelled with love for the Ecuadorian families who were able to create a home for their children with delicious food and joyous pastimes like soccer, while living without the modern tools we have come to take for granted in this country.

I witnessed families that were young and strong and bound tightly together in the rigors of life and the simple joys **that come** from simple living. They did it all without a flushing toilet or a warm shower.

I came home from Ecuador reluctantly, missing my experiences. Missing the hostel we found in Quito, on a beautiful maple-lined street, where we had a clean room and breakfast for seven dollars a night. Missing the music and the beautiful crafts available in the open air markets. Missing the discomfort that I learned to embrace, love and appreciate. Have you ever had an experience like that? One that makes you come home happy to see your house, no matter what state of disarray you find it in? I did it today. I worked in a doctor's office, strapped to a desk, being of service, doing everything I could. I came home to a very messy house, to children I missed, happy to be there. I came home happy to prepare dinner.

Recently, I met a guy named Gabe on an airplane who survived an Army tour in Iraq. He told me that the concept I have described here is called "embrace the suck". He told me he learned to appreciate things like the sweltering heat in the tent with dirt floors. He described the art of finding the good in the most horrid situations. Just go there, embracing the suck so you can make it home and love every problem home life has for you. A cracked foundation, septic system leak, dented car will never be a problem to you if you have had the opportunity to get uncomfortable and embrace the suck.

I advise you to go to a very uncomfortable place, embrace the suck while you are there, and come home with different perspective all together.

IN DEEP

There we stand, at the altar, in front of our family, friends, looking into each other's eyes and making promises about the future while not really knowing how it will unfold or what kind of people we will be when we encounter sickness and heath, richness or poverty, better times or worse. So, down the road, we have changed into different people. We have metamorphosed into fathers and mothers. Our relationship becomes more efficient and less emotional, and inevitably, we feel disconnected, discontent, lonely, and confused.

We may even feel angry, betrayed, unloved and unappreciated. We seek solace. We seek comfort. If we are uncomfortable being vulnerable with our spouse, we seek it elsewhere. We get into trouble.

In marriage, we get confused and let the boundaries between husband and wife blur. We think of our spouse as us. We think of ourselves as one. We are hard on ourselves and hard on our spouse. We lose compassion, the ability to forgive human weakness, the inevitability of making mistakes. We get bruised and grow fearful. We harden and turn cold. We shut down and stop talking. We forget to voice our needs without anticipating what the response might be. We manifest failure.

I have seen divorce. I have experienced it as a child, four times by my mother, whom I adore. I know that marriage is hard. The way I see it is this. At the inception of marriage, we know enough about each other to make a judgment call about the future, but we are not static. We are all constantly changing and growing. We cannot expect our partners to be exactly the same from day to day, they and we, have the right to grow and evolve.

I feel like I am just getting to know my husband of nine years. I do not feel that I know him completely and I never take for granted that he is an interesting, desirable person who chooses on a daily basis to spend his life with me. He is not "mine"; I do not own him. His body is his and I am fortunate that he chooses to share it with me, as I choose to share mine with him. Our marriage is an exploration. As the years are passing, I feel that the roots of our feelings are growing, deeper, stronger. I am not afraid of infidelity. I appreciate my husband, look at him from the perspective of other women and let him know how handsome, sexy, loving, thoughtful and wonderful he is. He also verbalizes more and more his appreciation and affection for me. Over time, we know each other more and enjoy the commingled experience of being together and parenting our children.

What happens, though, when we encounter real hurdles? What happens when one of us gets sick? Really sick? Terminally ill? How do we cope? How do we hold ourselves together and take care of ourselves so we can take care them? How do we make sense of financial instability, infidelity, addictions? How do we survive as individuals so that the marriage will? Can we come out of such a conflict intact? Can we come out stronger? I think we can.

I have hope, I have confidence that if we look only at ourselves, at our part, and are able to feel compassion for our partner, as much compassion as we would provide to a friend, we can survive. If we can see each other as individuals on unique journeys, and remember to take care of ourselves first, so that we are not neglected, we can thrive.

LUST FOR LIFE

Tomorrow morning I will leave my house at two AM, pack four kids in the car and drive to LAX for a six am flight across the country. I will spend seven days in a large house with my parents, sisters, their husbands and ALL of our eleven kids. We will eat together, swim together, make messes and clean up. There will be tantrums and sunburns, singing and poetry. We will write letters and have a talent show, eat and over-eat. Some of us will be cranky at times, maybe get our feelings hurt, but we will be together. As a family. I have a lust for life. I want to both devour it and savor it delicately. I get distracted as I pack because Clarissa, the kitten, walks by me, brushing her lean teenage cat body against my leg. I have to take a moment to hold her, scratching behind her ears, feeling the rumbling purr.

I will be away from my desk for three weeks. After a week on the beach, I jet off with my kids and meet up with my husband for two weeks in Ireland. He has set us up for an adventure that includes a fifteenth century single-family castle and a small village cottage. We like to live as if we were a part of a place, a part of a time, not visitors, passing through on the fringe. It will be an experience full of sensations I haven't yet had, yet already feel so familiar. I will have stories to tell anecdotes to report, musings and incidents that will inevitably change me for the better. I have a lust for life.

What kind of adventure do you want to have? Will it be a tropical romance with your caresses coming from a warm and gentle breeze? Will your adventure be tough and rugged, hiking in the badlands, grit between your teeth, fossils on your mind and nowhere near a shower? Or will it be rich with ancient art and culture in a two thousand year old city that takes you back in time with the first steaming bite of it's cuisine?

GO THERE

You never know how it's going to unfold. You think you do. You say "no" to things, anticipating the outcome. You think you'll be too stressed. That it will be too hard. You never know what's around the corner. What pieces of your life will come together with that unforeseen experience, with that person you sat next to on the plane? You just don't know what an experience will hold until you put your feet, your heart and your soul there. Open and ready for it. Don't let fear dictate where your path takes you. Set the anticipation, the fear, the anxiety and preconceived ideas aside. Walk in blank, happy, open, willing and fearless.

Fear can be such a paradox. It can tighten your muscles, shorten your breath, make your heart race, stifle your voice, stop you short of acting, inhibit your experiences and sabotage your successes. Fear can kill you before the thing you are afraid of has a chance to. I used to have nightmares of all the things I was terrified of: great white sharks eating me whole, men chasing me, trying to hurt or kill me, my boyfriend cheating, my husband communing with his ex-wife, my children in danger, nuclear weapons being deployed.

I have had to face all of these fears in my subconscious and realize, in the process of dreaming, that the fear is potentially more harmful than the actual thing of which I am fearful. I am very much aware of my mind's ability to manifest my reality, and so I don't entertain these fears in my waking hours. Ever. I am not afraid of identity theft, car jacking, burglary, earthquake, tsunami, fire, etc. I figure, I'll have the tools to deal with any situation that may arise and I'll keep with me my attitude, loving nature and sense of humor at all times.

Hey, I know this lifetime is relatively short and I'm willing to risk being uncomfortable for the exchange of a rich, experiential life. As I'm getting older, I realize my fear is diminishing. Victims create themselves with their fear. I don't think I will ever be one. As I think about my marriage, any fears I may have carried with me up till now, have cleared, like morning fog.

I hope to share this power with you. Just for today, I ask you to erase any and all fears or doubts you may have. What would you do without the fear? How will you react to a situation without the fear? How will you pursue your dreams without the fear? How will you interact with your partner without the fear?

As a gift to yourself, say yes today, where you might rather say no. Let go of the fear of what you think an experience will hold and just walk into it. Keeping the smile on your face. If nothing else, you may come out of it with a story to tell.

FULL

Scientifically, I can tell you that the full moon, because of its position in opposing the sun, pulls the oceans (and everything else) in its gravitational exchange. The tides are more extreme during a full moon and even more so during the new moon. Evolutionarily, the tidal fluctuations were probably responsible for life emerging from the oceans and populating land, as it allowed oceanic life the opportunity to evolve mechanisms of survival outside of water.

Spiritually, the full moon amplifies intentions and actions. Whatever you do during the full moon, whatever your intentions… the moon will intensify the effects. My daily goals have been to let go of judgment, annoyance, fear, struggle, and any negativity. I have navigated through a whirlwind of travel with children, happy, content and relatively stress free. But… my inner dialogue has played a part in helping me let go of certain things. Conflict keeps rising up in me in the form of annoyance with some people.

I read a profound statement that illuminated the solution to this problem. It was to imagine that person, or any for whom you foster any negativity, and hold them in your heart as perfect. Perfect where they are, as they are. My inner dialogue and exercise has gone something like this…. I struggle with my feelings of annoyance by telling myself that the person bugging me is perfect, just where he/she is.

To achieve nirvana is to ease all suffering. The great thing about this is that you have the power within you to suffer or to not suffer. Even in difficulty and in pain, our mind and our heart can be serene. I do not have to suffer. I can exchange my annoyance for love if I choose, and in the action of thinking this, I am bathed in serenity. I swear it works!

Of course, it is a bit more difficult to apply this technique when the subject of annoyance is your two small children arguing in the back seat of the car over a plastic tiger while you are trying to navigate a crowded freeway.... but, the goal for me is to keep on trying.

Next time the moon is full or new, notice this. Make your intentions and actions as powerful as they can be and choose serenity over suffering.

VACATION

I'm taking a break from stress. Clutter in the living room, shoe collections in the hallway, toys, papers and junk mail will all have to wait for my return. Grandma will get your cereal, auntie will wipe your nose, cousins will watch you swim. Mommy needs a break. I am forced to let hours pass doing nothing but sit and gaze. I am relinquishing the urge to accomplish something in the spare thirty minutes that would be a project at home. I am on vacation and I need the break.

I will soak up the warmth, the sweet sounds of the ocean waves and the kids frolicking in them. I am taking advantage, resting my hands and recharging my battery. My creative and healing energies are being amplified in their slumber. Dreaming energy connecting to where I am needed. I never knew the warmth of the Atlantic Ocean, the fine, silky sand. I was raised in the Pacific, cold by comparison, laden with kelp and grasses, tar stuck to my feet. The Atlantic is a caress, gentle and calming, soothing and inviting. I am on vacation. My mind rests, allowing my other senses just to take it in, whatever it may be.

Recharging your own energy levels is critically important. Asking yourself, your heart, what it desires each day and doing your best to nurture it, is the key to finding and keeping your blissful state. This is not selfish. This is smart. This act of giving to your heart, feeding it love, kindness and joy is what allows you to turn to the world with a heart that is loving, kind and joyful every day.

PRESENCE

It was sometime four or five thousand years ago that people created the stone circles that are in present day Ireland. I once visited one that had a center stone and two outer circle stones line up with the arc of the sun during the summer solstice. This stone circle meant something, served a purpose, brought people together in ceremony or reverence. It was a monument of some kind.

We have but a short time to make our mark. We all do. Some of us do it loudly and boldly, knowing we will leave an impression. Some of us are quiet and stealth in our passing through life, but pass nonetheless. We have presence- now.

We breathe. We have the opportunity to create, to feel, to experience or to create experiences. We are alive. We have this gift. Do you feel it? Your skin tingles with the touch of your own hand. If nothing else, we have the wealth of this moment. This breath. This opportunity. What would *THEY* give for what you have? This opportunity. What will you make of your today?

LOUD AND CLEAR

My throat had been hurting badly for over two weeks. Badly enough for me to see my internist who cultured me for strep but said it was probably allergies. To swallow was painful and my voice was beginning to reverberate. My friend, who had seen success with reiki, scheduled me an appointment. I met with the reiki practitioner, who, with her tender touch, worked my chakra system, channeling universal healing energy through my meridian.

My throat chakra was misaligned. No surprise. I was told that I needed to speak my anger. "But I can't- I don't have anger- only love, compassion, empathy..." Tears began to stream down my face. Fuck. I have anger. Unexpressed, of course. God damn it. I hate anger. I hate annoyance. I hate intolerance. I hate the weakness that comes with these shallow emotions. I hate having them. O.K., I was willing, am willing to admit my imperfections and express my (cough) anger. Ohh, that means fessing up to my deep, old wounds from my childhood when my father left my sisters and I with only a child support check and holiday cards signed "love, Dad" to mark his paternal contribution. He had two more children, whom I can truthfully say that I have slept under the same roof with fewer than fourteen times.

These children went on family vacations and had their father present at graduations and other important occasions. Not that I am jealous of them. I am not. I am only disappointed in my father for choosing to step aside and not partake in a difficult life as a father to three beautiful, strong women in addition to his two youngest children.

As a stepmother, I know first hand that divorce makes parenting far more challenging than it already can be. It is a challenge

44

for those of us willing to get down and dirty to stand by our children, for their sake, even if it makes us uncomfortable, uneasy, unsettled and unhappy. Even if it makes us cry, we should be there for our kids. He has no excuse; he should have been there for us. He wasn't. I'm angry. But maybe a little bit less, now that I've written the words. I am healing. My throat pain has eased, recovering from my stifled cry. Using my voice. Speaking loud and clear. Even if the words aren't pretty.

SERENITY IN THE CHAOS

You try and you try to gets things done, to complete, to achieve, to have success, but there are always delays, mishaps, roadblocks, hurdles and unforeseen mud holes that you find yourself falling into. The day, of course, is not long enough to feed and clothe the children, feed and clothe myself, unload the dishwasher so I can load it, clean up the kitchen so I can cook, feed the ten animals breakfast before lunchtime, log on to my e-mail, log on to the websites where I have an anticipated presence, create things on the computer, create jewelry at my desk, print out stone properties, package and mail things out, write bills and mail them on time, listen to voicemail, answer the phone, answer the cell phone, break up the fighting children, feed them lunch, take them to local spots of enrichment, rotate the laundry, unload and load the dishwasher, pick up the debris field in every room, have a meaningful relationship, be a good friend, think of others, make sure I'm taking care of myself, write this essay, take pictures, get pictures printed, put the prints in albums, update the baby books, clean out the closets, prepare for a garage sale, take a nap, quiet my mind.....That's not even the end of the list, but it's a start.

I know this is a common issue among women, who tend to have a knack for mentally cataloging things that need to be done, tended to, addressed, dealt-with. It must be part of the genetic double X that makes us acutely aware of the list of things to do. I suspect that the XX makes us feel a twinge of responsibility in making sure it all gets done.

My hope for you, as well as for me, is that we find all of our chores completed by some fairy or angel, husband or child, or, that what remains undone for now, does not irritate us or nag us with it's

46

incompleteness. Let us learn the art of prioritizing and maintain a peaceful heart and a sense of humor as we exist serenely in the midst of chaos.

THERE IS NO RIGHT WAY

The first time I took physics in college I struggled. My professor was a young Indian man who solved physics problems on his dry erase board as if it was so obvious that the problem should be solved the way he solved it. He taught with haste, annoyance and seemingly, just because he had to. I tried to learn by following his steps, by doing it his way, by memorizing the procedure that he so casually presented to his class. I didn't learn. I achieved a less than passing grade. I felt mighty stupid and quite the failure.

I repeated physics and learned much more than just physics in the process. I'm not sure if it was my next professor's passion for teaching or my own maturity, but I figured out that in physics, there was more than one way to solve a problem. I had to come up with my own methods of breaking down the problem, solving each component as I understood it, and arriving at the conclusion my own way. I didn't have to use the same technique as anyone else, as long as I understood what needed to be done and came up with a plan for getting there. I ended up with the top grade in a class of eighty some students and a renewed love for physics.

This lesson has stuck with me. I am a problem solver and don't give up easily. I rarely back away from a difficult situation or a seemingly impossible task. I tend to say "yes" even when I don't know how something is going to come together or where the financial backing will come from. I find things that are lost because I will not give up looking.

Here is my method. If you have an obstacle or a goal, write down what you know, write down what you want to know then figure out how to get there. This formula can work for almost any situation in life to get you from where you are to where you want to go. Anything. There are no limits. The power of intention works because you put that intention out there in your actions, in your beliefs and in your encounters with others towards a particular goal.

Think about the guy in Canada who traded a red paperclip for a house (after many trades and some choice items for barter). His intentions were clear. He asked for what he wanted in every transaction. He modeled what intention and belief and hard work can do for you. He inspired hope. I also wish to inspire hope.

The hardest part is knowing what you want or what you need. Once you figure that out, there is no right way (or wrong way) to how you get there. You have more to work with than you think in order to get it.

CONFIRMATION

I was once told that I don't ask for help enough from my angels. It's true. I don't ask for help. This, of course, is not good. I was told that my angels are there, waiting, willing, happy to help, at any time, but I have to ask. I have to ask.
I was told that I get confirmation from my angels in the form of chills down my spine, shivers and goose bumps. I took this information and have been applying it. It's worth asking just for the feeling of electricity surging up and down my spine in response to a question I have asked from my angels.

Another reliable source told me that I have a lot of angels supporting me. Over twenty. A literal support team. I have decided that I am going to engage their talents more frequently than I have been. I am going to trust their abilities and go at whatever's in front of me with the full knowledge that the team is on it.

I can and will do so much more now with my angel support staff in action. I'm letting the stubborn independence go, in exchange for the angelic team approach. I figure, that if I have that many souls connected to me then I must have some pretty important work to do and I'd best get my ego out of the way and get to it. I asked for financial flow. I am getting it. I asked for direction and instructions on how I work with my stones. I am getting it. I am open to receiving it. It is my job now to remind you to do the same thing.

Imagine that you have a support team devoted solely to you. Imagine that their greatest happiness comes in loving and helping you to do your life's work. Imagine that you can accomplish anything. Know that you are heard. Know that you are adored. Know that you are integral to this planet at this time. Know that. Feel the shivers? Ask a question. Ask for guidance. Feel the shivers?

BREATHE IN JOY

My sisters and I created magic last weekend. We envisioned, planned and executed a weekend in New York City to surprise our mother in honor of her sixtieth birthday. We made a miracle happen. We found care for our eleven children. We financed our trip by manifesting the cash. We experienced NYC without blisters on our feet, without rain, without terrorism. We were gifted with cupcakes from Magnolia Bakery, Grey Gardens; the musical, and hot corned beef from the Broadway Deli. We ran, laughing, down the hall of the hotel with bras on our heads, flirted with bus drivers and saw orbs in the photos we took in the subway tunnels. It truly was a magical weekend for me with my sisters and my mother and her friends. I am rich. I am full. I am satisfied and I am happy.

I invite you to manifest as much fun or more for yourself.

TEACHERS

They have something to teach. It's something I have been willing to study my whole life. How to nap, how to ask for what you want, how to be persistent in the asking, how to say," no, I don't care for that", and without hesitation, they know how to say, "pet me!" I have always been attracted to cats. I have five. They are like magnets to my iron, pulling me away from my task, drawn to their exposed belly, their sleepy smile. They know how to savor the sunlight and the leafy, dappled shade. They know how to be clean and how to get really dirty.

One of my cats, large and grey, a beautiful male, sleeps in my lavender garden. I pick him up and he smells like my favorite flower, clean, bright and honest. I can't really explain it other than a pure fascination, a lifelong attraction to the feline form, an admiration and a love.

I have a friend who resonates with dogs. She says dogs are her favorite people, loyal, honest, reliable. I am certain she is not alone. When one looks at the animals surrounding us as teachers, there are lessons to be learned from each and every one. I think maybe it's because they speak without words, *showing us how.*

If you believe in animal totems, or have studied animal cards, you notice that the animal teaches us through it's actions translated and applied to our world. We can learn and discover so much about ourselves by observing animals. As teachers, they give the most sage advice without ever speaking a word.

YOU CAN'T HATE YOURSELF

I have been really busy. Demands for my time and energy have stretched me thin. Well not actually, I am actually being stretched fat. My children have needed me, my creative urges consume any scraps of time. I am drowning in clutter in my home and still haven't recovered from a long summer of travel. I am running on fumes and still have so much on my plate that needs my attention.

I realized the other night, after consuming a substantial quantity of raw cookie dough, that I was not allowed to hate myself, for A. Eating sugar, which I have been trying to give up, and B. Indulging in the forbidden substance in such a gluttonous fashion.

I wanted to hate myself. I was leaning toward the old habit of self-hatred, which is a set up for more "bad" behavior. No matter how appalling the act was, the thing I could not allow myself to do was to hate myself for the weakness that defines me as human.

It is really the thing that binds us. We inevitably, on a daily basis make mistakes, do things wrong, hurt people's feelings, trip up in our goals, show ourselves as vulnerable and imperfect. Not one of us is immune to the pitfalls of the human condition. Some mistakes are huge, and made very public, some are tiny and known only to us, our little secret, like the cookie dough. Having grown up with recovering alcoholics, I know about making mistakes and how important it is to find compassion and forgiveness first for yourself, so you can make amends where they are required to be made.

I can only imagine the effect of every earthly individual coming to terms with their imperfect nature, and offering compassion, first to themselves, then to all those around them. Can you imagine the power in that?

Whatever you have done, whatever it is, I hope you will forgive yourself and let it be considered a lesson in being human. It will not be the last mistake you make, but it may be the last one of that kind. I can't say that I won't eat raw cookie dough again. I can say that I will not hate myself if I do indulge, for that would ruin the sweetness of the experience.

HOW TO MAKE IT ALL FUN

We switched cars, my husband and I, so he could take my Toyota hybrid on a long day-trip to Monterey and I could tootle around town, doing motherly things, in his non-hybrid car. I dropped the kids off at their respective schools. I actually thought to myself, "this car is like driving a roller skate with metal wheels", as I felt every bump in the road, every crack. Later, as I exited the freeway on my way to a meeting and I felt the telltale thud-thud-thud-thud, I knew why the car drove like that. It pretty much *was* a roller skate with a metal wheel. I was, miraculously, never annoyed.

I was happy my husband was safely driving my car, and that my kids were in school so I had the time to wait for the Auto Club of Southern California. I was not annoyed, alarmed or peeved. I left my car, walked to my meeting, and when it was over, arranged to have a nice man in thick gloves change my tire. While I waited, I took some photographs, as I always carry my camera in my purse. I took some beautiful shots of flowers, sun-dappled leaves, a statue of two doves kissing. It was an altogether lovely morning. Sure, I wasn't able to write a essay that morning, or make a belly chain, but I did receive some much needed time to just breathe, enjoy the view of the mountains in the morning light and just spend a few minutes with myself.

I believe situations like this one happen for a reason. I think if we can look at even the seemingly tough situations as opportunity, we learn that it *can* all be fun!

THE EVOLUTION OF DOUBT

Raising children provides a bit of an opportunity to study human nature. I have the privilege of being a stepmother of two girls who are now in the mid teen and early adulthood stages of their lives, so I really have observed the course of self power that evolves as we grow.

My small children, an observant and stubborn three year old and a dreamy, distractable six year old, serve as my early childhood models. They are demanding of what they want. They ask for big and small, dream of trips to Disneyland and swimming with dolphins in Hawaii. They manifest with their words and in their art. They do not doubt in their ability to get what they want. My teenage children are at the stage of being afraid to want. They tell me, they cannot have strong desires because their fear of not receiving or not achieving them is too great. Failure would be too painful. Fear of *not* getting is motivation for not asking, not wanting.

The oldest, who is in college now, expressed her fears about not getting into the right college from the first semester of her freshman year in high school. Her motivation for learning was not to learn, but to earn the grade that would provide the best chance of getting into the most competitive schools. It was her belief that students who didn't achieve a 4.0 grade point average were doomed to sub-standard collegic experiences.

When it came time to apply, she dared to not want any one college too much. The fear of not getting what she wanted was greater than the hope that she would achieve her goal. Her fear was confirmed when she auditioned for the UCLA school of theater, a very small, highly competitive program, and vocalized a passionate desire to be accepted into this program and was very disappointed when she did not get accepted. In hindsight, she is now a student at a small, highly respected liberal arts college in the Pacific Northwest and has been very active in their theater department.

I am now experiencing the same doubtful behavior emerging from my second stepdaughter. Now a high school freshman, she is more mature and self-aware than most her age, but still limits her future with her verbal communication of doubt. I don't know exactly how she feels, but what she verbalizes to me is the same fear her sister had about the grades and the colleges. She insisted to me that she was not as smart as I thought she was, implying that I didn't know the real her.

Of course, this is all a bunch of "dark matter" which clouds the truth and weighs down the heart to the point of self-doubt or even self-loathing. Being an optimist and a full believer and subscriber in the law of attraction, I prefer to see my children in the stage of believing in miracles and asking for the world.

I know, from experience, that if there is something you really want, you can and will have it. You may have to take many steps to get there and never accept failure as an option, but you will have it. It may not fall into your lap, you may not know how it will come to be yours you may have to work very hard, persevere, never give up, but if you believe that it will happen, it *will* happen.

I used to write notes to the universe asking for very specific things. My husband started out as a journal entry with qualities listed and, "he " literally, showed up as a blind date. My child was a request made on a strip of paper placed in my wish box. She came to me as a positive pregnancy test on my thirtieth birthday. Our house, which we wanted to buy but couldn't, came to us after a request was made to the universe, in writing, as a wish in my wish box. My daughter was six weeks old when we signed the papers. Over and over I have made requests. I know that for me there are no limits to what I can have, so I am shooting BIG. I am shooting for the elimination of self-doubt of all people. I am aiming for the birth of self-forgiveness

61

and compassion for all people. I am envisioning the feeling of existing in a world where there are no limits to what we can achieve.

I'm not sure where the doubt comes from. The instructions to limit your dreams, to quiet your desires and to shrink yourself down to a smaller size altogether, occurs somewhere between childhood and adulthood. Imagine the greatness that would never have happened if all people doubted in their abilities, gave up on their dreams and just shrunk to a level of "normal" that kept them free from the pain of failure. Imagine all that would have been lost and all that could be lost if this were a universal phenomenon. The pattern of people who have achieved what we perceive of as great is that they dreamed and worked and did not fear, nor did they give up in the face of failure. They defied the evolution of their doubt.

SECRET

In dreams my guardian angel whispers it to me. Laughing, hiding her mouth so I only see her eyes. It is fun for her to know this and keep it hidden from me. She says it is like a present that you can unwrap at any time. The secret is... we create our own experience. In essence, we are driving our own destiny. We can play with the future. We can create wealth, poverty, heath or illness. We can create love and unity or discord and disruption. As souls in physical form, we are capable of attracting whatever we want. We have a hard time knowing what that is, and even second-guess ourselves when we do know what we want. We are afraid of being wrong. We are afraid to ask. We won't even vocalize our wishes sometimes because we believe they could never happen. We don't always trust ourselves.

I have, since childhood, seen the future as a present. Wrapped up for me to open and enjoy. My life has really been like that. I enjoy it. I, of course, have a list of manifestations that I am willing into action. Money - so much that I have plenty to share, an easement of the self criticism that hinders the manifestational abilities of my loved ones, health and a healthy appreciation of the miraculous machine that is my body, and of course, world peace through a very specific visualization of my limitless heart energy wrapping around the planet twice, empowering each individual with the gift of self love and compassion.

I dream big. I don't limit myself. *How else can I propel myself to the status of benevolent and powerful healer of the planet?*

LOVE

It is such a common word. Thrown around casually or withheld in discomfort. It is simple and I think it is the key to heal, nurture, save, reconcile, forgive, rebuild, open up, step out and really live fully. Love. Love lets you crank up the Charlie Brown Christmas music in your car as you wait in line at school to collect your child so the parents around you can hear it too. Love allows you to heal the horrific wounds of war by allowing perpetrators to provide and victims to accept an acknowledgment and an apology.

Love of life gives us the sight to see all that is beautiful, to feel all that is joyful in our everyday experiences. The full moon shimmering a path on the placid, black water. Love displaces greed. Love displaces fear. Fear that there won't be enough. Fear that if we give too much it will open a door to theft. Love provides an impenetrable armor against the most deadly attack. Love softens the blow of infidelity, betrayal, the human weakness that we are all capable of. Love of ourselves first strengthens our hearts and readies them to face any and all challenges.

When we have love for ourselves and we nurture our passions, we are whole and cannot be shattered. Our souls are unbreakable. Love allows us to float in joy by attracting more of the same wherever we go. Love creates itself, infectious and communicable. Love opens doors and hearts. Love melts frigidity. Love changes people. Love reverses tragedy.

Give it to yourself. Give it away. The supply is endless. The more you use the more there is. Give a drop and receive a wave. LOVE. I mean it.

YOU MAY NOT BELIEVE THIS

I love my body. I love the way it can change at my whim. I love taking the mental tour, riding the course of the blood through my heart, picturing the rhythmic, steady beating, pumping. When I used to donate blood regularly, I used to be amazed at how warm the bag was, as it filled, propped heavily next to me. Warm and comforting, waiting to share it's nurturing energy with someone else. I love my body and how I can both give and receive touches, to my legs, my belly, feeling the softness of the skin, or appreciating the rough that needs smoothing. I love the way the curves can be sculpted and that at any time in one's life, the body can be changed. It can wax and wane in size, like the moon. It can recover from famine and obesity. It can grow more muscle and gain strength at any site where muscle exists.

This body allows me to hear music and soar in my imagination with the sounds. I can savor foods and have a thirst that when quenched, tastes the best water ever. I can smell and see, touch and hear. I can move and feel the stretch of a tired muscle, take comfort in the feeling of my straight hair pulled between two fingers.

I love my body and the opportunity it affords me. To curl up in comfort under a warm and heavy blanket for a guilt-free nap in the afternoon. To retreat into my mind for trips into the past or the future, rich with possibility. The body is a gift, in any state. Pain, as I have experienced in childbirth, can serve so much as a pendulum. In labor, the absence of pain is pleasure. In debilitating disease, the pain is feeling, it is experience and I imagine, it allows one insights into realms unreachable without it.

In any form, the body is a gift, a wonder and a delight. There is good in it all and in all its possibilities. I ask you, today, to look at your body with different eyes, seeing it for what it is: a miracle. Talk to your organs, your heart, lungs, kidneys, intestines, your muscles, blood vessels, brain and bones. Notice how cuts heal and change is always possible. Notice how food is digested and water is absorbed. See your precious body for what it is, and LOVE it, give it the gift of your appreciation, your care and watch how it responds.

TRANSFORMATION

Metamorphosis. I am going through a transformation. Many of us are. We are shedding our outer layers, peeling away the old skin. We are physically changing, painfully at times. We have been sick, depressed, unnerved. We are shifting, shedding, growing and it hurts. I imagine it as a metamorphosis. We re learning new skills, waking up to find hidden talents and feel passion that does not yet fit into our daily lives. We are not alone. I bet you know what I'm talking about.

I have been sick for six weeks. My brain is foggy, not sharp. My motivation for certain tasks is lacking. It's hard for me to slow down to allow the shift to occur. I can't say that I have been unhappy though. I feel hopeful and inspired. I have visions of my future self, confident, luminous and beautiful in all ways. My family seems to be growing ever closer as the months turn into years, as if we are very much on the same path. When I see friends struggling or suffering in pain, I visualize the shift happening in them. The breaking of old habits and the re-tuning of body instruments to play a totally different musical score. Happy to be here, as always, even in the struggle, even in the exhaustion, even in the fog. I am happy.

PRESENTS

The day was warm, like a caress. It left me with my shoulders bared and comfortable in a skirt with bare feet. It was truly spring in Santa Barbara, eighty-five with bulbs emerging in bursts of green and a warm breeze even in the shade. Present. I am and it was. I even wrote a thank you note- in advance- to the universe for the presents to come in the remainder of the year. I know I will not be disappointed. I always get what I ask for. I am grateful for the impact I will make on the world, the lives I will change. I thanked the universe for my healthy, beautiful, fit body, for the adventures we would have as a family on our travels and for my husband and his prosperous business. I am a wealthy, content woman who dares to devour each day with lust and appreciation for the smallest distraction. If today were a gift, it would have been wrapped in cornflower blue paper and tied with a lime green and fuchsia striped bow. It would have been one of many many gifts that I have come to appreciate and share.

Write your thank you note. Deliver it. Move through your days as if the gift has already come.

DOING YOUR BEST

I try to do my best every day. I am careful about how I interact with people, trying to add positive energy to seemingly minute interactions. I try to do the right thing in my work. I give as much if not more than I receive. I am generous and trusting with people, I believe in bringing out the best in people by expecting it. I am as loving and caring with my stepchildren as I am with my biological ones. They are all mine and none of them are mine. I say "yes" when someone needs help. I step up to the plate, even when the job is tough. I do the best that I can, not always succeeding like a super-mom would, but by trying and being willing to fail, rather than by not trying at all.

My sister, Stephanie thinks I should write a book about how to be a good stepmother. She says that she uses me as an example of "how-to" with her friends who need some perspective into the world of raising someone else's kids. What I have is the perspective of someone who has been step-parented.

I have had one stepmother and four stepfathers. I was a child born of the marriage of children. My sisters and I looked up to our parents, expecting them to be right and good, secure and strong, with full confidence that they were all of these things. We trusted our stepparents to behave well too. We trusted them to love us, support us, support our relationship with the parent they were married to and the parent they were filling in for. In trust, we were frequently let down.

I learned how to be a good stepmother by remembering what it feels like to be a stepchild. I hold my older girls' mother in very high esteem. I am willing to support her in any way that I can, because I know how much I loved my mother and wanted her to be held in the highest esteem. There can be no rationalizing about why a parent is not a good one, in the eyes of a child. Nature makes parents perfect people in the eyes of their children. All misdeeds are forgivable. And so, as a stepmother, my job is to join my girls in the love they have for their mother.

Children are children for such a short time but carry the moldings of childhood into the solidification of their adult lives. Being loving, supportive, kind, nurturing, firm and trustworthy as a stepparent, is the right thing to do. I don't distinguish between the lines of marriage and bloodlines. In our family, I like to include my stepdaughters' sister, from their mother's subsequent marriage, in our important family events. I can so easily make her happy and provide her with great childhood memories, just by treating her as I would want to be treated.

My father never included my sisters and me on a vacation with his new family. I do the opposite. I don't take a trip without all of my kids. As an adult, I also have been blessed by the example of my amazing stepfather, who parents like I do. He loves my sisters and me and all of our children like we were his own. He treats us with respect, kindness, generosity and he adores our mother.

Step parenting comes with the bonus of having a big family without having to go through all of those pregnancies. I love being a part of a big crazy family. We fill all seven seats of the car, play board games, take big, memorable vacations where somebody inevitable complains too much about the food, or how boring it all was, but I truly love it.

Whether they love me as much as I love them is not important. I am sure my work will show its value when it comes time for these kids to become parents. They won't have to resort to "just do the opposite". They will know just what to do to make the experience of being a family as precious as it can possibly be.

GIFTS

Sometimes the gift is something you didn't want. It is something you didn't ask for.

I wrote this great essay this morning about seizing the day, living in the now and really appreciating this day- the only moment you really have- right now. I wrote all this stuff about not projecting your fear or anticipatory judgment on what your day hands you. Every moment of every day is a gift and some of those gifts come completely out of the blue and some are gifts you have asked for and worked towards. I said that you shouldn't shy away from the surprises. Don't think that you know what the box contains or whether or not you are going to love it once you try it on.

I said all this stuff and then the whole essay got lost. I realized the essay was for me. The gift was mine. I know this, because minutes after my essay was erased I received a call that could lead me to a new career. I was excited but began to feel scared with the anticipation of how this new development would impact my life. I was doing exactly what I advised my readers to avoid. The message was for me. The gift was for me.

I am so grateful for the presents of my present even when they scare me or annoy me. I love it all. In all my imperfection, I am able to cheer on others but left sometimes doubting myself. Life is funny. I can do nothing but chuckle.

LIVING LIKE THERE IS NO TOMORROW

I remember sometime in my late teens, after buying my first car, a 1974 blue Volkswagen Bug, feeling a true sense of freedom. To me, it was the freedom of opportunity, the knowing of the eminent possibility that there were adventures to be had. I had friends then who shared my sense of freedom and adventure, and we made the most of out time together and our freedom in the form of cars and driver's licenses. It was the sense of freedom and the fire of our imaginations that we were high on. I remember thinking "why would anyone use drugs when life itself can make you feel so high?" I think that thought came on a night that we parked one of our cars at the end of the LAX runway off Vista Del Mar, in El Segundo, CA and felt the roar of the jumbo jets as they ascended into the sky from right above our heads.

Now that I am a mother, and a "stay-at-home" one at that, I like to have adventures with my kids. Santa Barbara is so full of the possibility for adventure that I sometimes am forced to piggy back one adventure on top of another just to take advantage of the cornucopia of possibility. One week in particular included a beached whale, and an adventure involving a B-17 Bomber.

The whale adventure began when my sister Stacy called to ask about the beached whale in Isla Vista. It jarred my memory of a radio blurb that morning about a beached sperm whale that I had heard but filed away somewhere in the back of my head for safekeeping.

Upon jarring the idea loose, I was determined to commune with this amazing creature of the deep, and called **my** friend Jill. "Hey, you wanna go on an adventure?" I asked. "Absolutely!" She replied. We didn't know exactly where we were going, for the whereabouts of the whale had not yet shown up in the news. I told her I'd heard it was on Isla Vista beach. She drove. I trust Jill's connection to nature. She connects with animals (or they connect with her), even though she denies this vehemently. It may be purely coincidental, but Jill drove us to I.V. and found us a parking place. We descended the nearest set of stairs to the beach and found that we were within visual range of a beached sperm whale.

There was a small crowd marveling at the amazing creature. Kieran, my daughter, said it looked like a big plucked chicken. It was an accurate description. The whale was wrinkled and pink. The kids were fascinated and tried to get close but the whale was caught in the slowly rising tide and moved in and out, as if still alive, raising its caudal fin occasionally with the bigger waves.

The kids were playing chicken with the carcass of the great sperm whale, chasing after it as the waves receded and running screaming back as the whale surged closer with the swell. It was wild and windy and I feared someone from our car was going to have a close encounter with decomposing whale tissue. I figured all was well though. This was, in fact an experience of communing with nature, wasn't it? When else could my kids get close enough to actually kiss a sperm whale if they so chose? It was a great moment. A great present of the present where we acted in the spirit of adventure for a moment of discovery.

The day after our kids had communed with the corpse of the great whale by playing "chicken" with it in the surf, we again were alight with the fiery spirit of adventure. The whale had drifted out with the tide the previous night and re-beached on a different beach. We took a picnic lunch down to a beach just south of where the whale had been the evening before. Again, I trusted Jill's natural ability to connect with wildlife and encouraged her to choose the beach. I was not disappointed. We finished eating our lunch and started walking down the beach.

We were rewarded almost immediately with the sight of a giant excavator digging a whale-sized hole for the black mound next

79

to it. There was a crowd of people around and as we got closer, we could see why. It was what whalers must have looked like, covered from chest to toe on yellow rubber pants, standing on top or inside the whale wielding huge, four-foot-long scalpels.

There was a scientific team performing a gross dissection. We had to cross a stream of whale blood to get to the up-wind side of the decomposing whale. The intestines were being extracted with the help of a large hook and I think I identified the huge black liver, a rare privilege for a bystander.

The following day, doing my duty as a field-trip driving parent, I joined my daughter's first grade class on a field trip to the Santa Barbara Airport where we were treated to the most exciting surprise... a World War II era B-17 Bomber, built in 1944 and in perfect condition. It was gleaming with its polished chrome-riveted body, with thirteen gunnery positions located throughout the plane. We were treated to a tour inside the plane.

I returned with my son for a second tour. From the inside, we could safely imagine our young, brave soldiers, knowingly putting their lives on the line, to man the war bird. We could even cross the catwalk in the belly of the plane to see where the bombs would be dropped as the huge doors opened exposing the runway below. It was a priceless experience.

Being open to adventure and exited by the constant prospect of it really keeps me living like there's no tomorrow.

LET DEATH BE A REMINDER

A good friend of mine wrote me last week to tell me that her husband's best friend had died suddenly of a brain aneurism during a spin class, something he loved to do. His name was Tim.

We are blessed or cursed with never knowing how long it will be, this precious opportunity to be "in body". It's funny, the way we pretend that it's never going to happen. We mourn a death, die a little ourselves when someone we love leaves us. But, as living organisms, death is the only inevitable we have. It is the one thing that we can safely predict, that all living things will reach an end to their lifetime and will nurture with their physical remains, or with the impact they have had on others, new or continued life.

Having kids means facing your fears about death. I talk to my kids about it, keeping a constant open dialogue, so they won't be afraid of it. I say, *"everything that is living will eventually die-everything and everybody has a life span. We do not know how long our life will be, because some things are just meant to remain a mystery"*.

Embedded in the message is the feeling that every day that we are alive should be a cherished gift and an opportunity to celebrate. When we do go, we will feel like we devoured life, appreciating every breath, every caress, every kiss, every sweet-smelling flower, every violet sunset, every golden sunrise. We will have lost sleep to witness meteor showers, soothing sick children, dancing and drinking too much, taking trans-oceanic flights to reach distant shores and new experiences. We will have experienced the rush of adrenaline from our first time driving fast, climbing high, sailing in a gale force and, of course, pushing ourselves in at least one amazing spin class.

We will have loved every second of this life, wasting little time. When our friends leave us, they give us the greatest gift. They remind us of the opportunities we have been blessed with by being born human.

Today, I honor Tim and I thank him for reminding me and so many others that I have this moment to savor, to devour and to submerse myself in, utilizing every sense to celebrate this day of my life. I thank Tim today for allowing his death to be my reminder to *live*.

ITS ONLY CALLED DROWNING IF YOU STOP WANTING TO LIVE

You know the saying, "Just trying to keep my head above water"? I have given up on that. My life has been so harried lately. I can't keep my head above water any more. I can't keep swimming with the same view ahead of me. I have taken a deep breath and succumbed to the depths and the blue of below the surface. It's only drowning when you give up and stop wanting to experience it all. I have given up trying to keep it all afloat and keep juggling the same tasks, keep going at the same frantic pace, keep doing the same heroic things. I am taking a lung full of air and diving in deep to see what I have been trying to avoid for so long. Maybe under the surface, it is paradise, and all this time I have been fighting against it.

To be completely open to life is to be willing to endure the inevitable pain associated with living fully. To take that lung full of air, feel the pain of doing something completely new and scary. Not just fighting to keep up the same old stuff, struggling to keep your head above water. I am doing it. Rolling with the waves, holding my breath like a free diver, taking in the new world before me. It's adventurous. It is risky. It is possibly going to get me into trouble that I cannot foresee. It is, at this very moment in time, FUN.

WANT TO BET?

I try not to doubt. I have always seen the fun in making things happen. Even seemingly impossible things do not thwart me. I fully enjoy the challenge of asking, scheming, seeing the problem through, working towards it as if it were going to happen etc. Sure, not everything comes to pass, but the important stuff always does and the rest is still unfolding as I continue to breathe in and out, in and out. It ain't over 'till it's over, and it's far from over from where I sit now. I am thoroughly annoyed by the pessimist.

I have teenagers, (with dreams), who use pessimism as a means to avoid disappointment. It drives me crazy to witness their self-limiting, self-inflicted bondage. They fear not achieving the goal more that they want to reach out and grab it. I am trying to teach them to use my technique, but its hard to turn fearful people into optimists. Still, I have an excellent track record and it's hard to say that it all came from chance.

My daughter Kieran is much like me. She manifests. She manifested a female orange tabby named Clarissa, whom she requested from the universe for her sixth birthday. Clarissa, born under a house in Pacific Palisades in March, was delivered to Kieran one week before her sixth birthday, exactly as she had requested. Kieran is patient. She makes her request, draws pictures, makes lists with her object of desire depicted in a requesting format, like an order. She did this many months ago in the form of a request for a baby chick. She asked me, "Mom, can I have a chick?". "Absolutely not!", I said. "We do not live on a farm, we don't have room for chickens". This request and dialogue was made more than once. I even went so far as to add, "You may have as many chickens as you want on your very own farm, when you are a grown up. But not here and not now."

Guess what I have in my back yard in a converted bunny hutch right now. One guess. Go on. Say it. You know what I am going to say, so just spit it out. Yes, you are correct. I have a chick. No Kieran has a chick, rapidly developing into a chicken. Her name is Henny. The way she came to us was so sly, so underhanded, that the universe literally got my husband Tom and I to go out of our way to secure her. I am sure someone is giggling somewhere right now at our predicament.

The story involved a baby quail found on the sidewalk on a windy spring evening, a chick purchased at the feed store to help rehabilitate it and subsequent demise of the quail. The chick's name became Henny.

The days turned into weeks and little Henny bonded with us, but especially with Kieran, and is now a young, very people-friendly hen. Again, I suspect that somewhere in the universe, someone is chuckling. I have instructed Kieran to not ask for any more animals for a while, or to add the caveat, "When I am much older" when making her requests to the universe. She is a powerful manifester and this I respect greatly. I would rather combat issues of abundance any day. The effects of doubt are much less fun to deal with.

PERFECTLY IMPERFECT

Last night I attended a great party. It may have been because there was music that left me no choice but to dance. I can still hear "m m m my Sharonna" playing in my head. It may have been great because there were lots of kids who knew each other and they went arm and arm running off to play tether ball and dodge ball together, far away from where I sat sipping wine and spearing salami wedges with a toothpick. It may have been because my husband, who generally dislikes socializing with anyone but his children actually wanted to stay for the entire party. I loved it for the people who were there, the perfect mix of late afternoon sun, a cool glass of Chardonnay and the opportunity for me to be there amongst it all.

I was amused by this guy at the party who tells me he's heard that there were people drinking wine at the Back to School BBQ that took place the evening before. He alerts me with an air of seriousness and doom-filled authority that this combination of alcohol meeting with lips, tongue and throat on the hallowed ground of a public school is not only illegal but also a felony. He tells me this in a manner meant to alarm me into action, now that I have taken on the role of PTA president of said school, but it doesn't alarm me. My response to him is "well I too was drinking wine, discretely of course, from a paper bag, directly out of the bottle". How could it ever be an action punishable by incarceration to be present within the sight of a hundred screaming children at the end of a very long week, with a receptacle of imbibment in hand, parental supervision galore, within walking distance from home? The guy said to me, "yeah, wouldn't it be a scandal for the PTA president to be taken away from school in handcuffs from the back to school BBQ?" My reply to him was "that wouldn't be the worst thing that could happen to me ". In fact, now that I think about it, it could actually be beneficial. It would release me from any future PTA positions as well as the current role of President.

I am really quite comfortable looking "bad" in public. I have figured out that being imperfect is not only *not* fatal but it is what we are supposed to do. Look at someone like Martha Stewart. Being perceived as perfect made her an easy target and pretty much earned her a vacation in a white-collar prison. Fortunately Martha, like many of us, knows that this type of humiliation will not kill you and can actually increase your levels of compassion for others.

There is a quote by Teilhard de Chardin, " You are not a human being in search of a spiritual experience, you are a spiritual being immersed in a human experience". And nothing spells human more than any form of public f**k up. So today, I encourage you to make a fool out of yourself. Please try to emphasize your perceived imperfections. Do something that would normally mortify you and see what happens. Laugh it off when you are obviously wrong, say "I'm sorry" even if it wasn't your fault. My new mantra is, *I reserve the right to be wrong.*

Please, for the sake of humanity, strive to be perfectly imperfect. You will not be alone.

MATURITY MEANS LETTING GO

I think I'm starting to get it. Letting go is really powerful. I used to worry excessively as a child, about everything. I even remember reading a saying that was posted on the ceiling above the orthodontist's chair that said, "Worry is like a rocking chair, it takes you back and forth but gets you nowhere". Profound. So, in my maturity, I have applied this idea of letting go to many things. I do not worry too much about things. I kind of don't even think about things I have to do until they are staring me right in the face. This is my secret to effortless public speaking. I try to let go of my expectations.

I see people hurting all the time because their expectations have not been met. I take Byron Katie's advice to "love what is", which really simplifies a lot. I try not to be attached to things, even things with sentimental value. Even memories, don't really need to be held on to. They will survive or they won't survive, and either way, it's really OK. I still have to remind myself to not feel guilt for things I have done, or haven't done. There could be nothing more stagnating than guilt to keep you from action. Imagine how many people have not shown their face again at an event, function, gathering or fill in the blank, even when they have wanted to, due to guilt. How stupid is that?

I have come to believe that as humans, it is our job to screw up, so if we are doing that, then good for us. No need for guilt. Pat yourself on the back if you have let someone down today and see if tomorrow you can do it differently.

Old people seem to get this. They know that only relationships matter. They tell you to "keep your house clean" and they aren't talking about the house you live in. They tell you that the small stuff doesn't matter and the things that get lost, broken or leave you are just things. They tell you that kids grow up, no matter what, and sometimes you just have to step back, let go and let them fail. Just like you did, remember?

Boy it feels good to let go. Try it! It lightens your heart and makes you feel a little bit giddy with the relief. Imagine the effect it could have on your worry lines!

YOU ONLY LIVE ONCE *OR A THOUSAND TIMES DEPENDING ON WHAT YOU BELIEVE*

Would you be surprised if I told you that part of my soul resides in a rock? Yeah, I know it sounds crazy, but I'm beginning to get it. The real stuff *sounds* crazy.

In this body, we sacrifice time on the planet for mobility. We can go anywhere, connect with anyone or any thing. Our lives are short, very short, but we can flit around and make our predestined connections. We have friends who have sacrificed mobility or will for time. Trees are connected to the grid through their roots. They may live for thousands of years, pulsing with life. They have to wait for you to come to them. Listen when they call you. Respect the call, connect and exchange, as you will.

Rocks can live for billions of years. They sacrifice their connection when they become a fragment, but they then have mobility. They can carry stored information, or possibly more.

Imagine the possibility that a physical blueprint, something like DNA through a drop or two of blood, for example, could be downloaded into a crystal for storage into the future. The concept isn't as crazy as it sounds. Amber is a stone that can possibly preserve genetic material for hundreds of millions of years through the blood of mosquitoes that get preserved in the sap that hardens into the amber. What if a crystal preserves information in a vibrational sort of way, like a memory. Many people who work with crystals for healing, note that certain formations can be used and accessed as record-keeper crystals.

I had an experience with a large Crystal Quartz formation that was straight out of a science fiction movie. I bent down to admire this beautiful stone in someone's home and was inclined to place my

92

hands on either side of it. When the closed circuit was created, I began to feel a surge of emotion, like I had been reunited with someone I had been missing for a very long time. The only way I could describe the feeling was to say that the crystal held a memory of the true *me*, **a more complete** *me*.

Even though it sounds crazy, I believe it is possible that I stored myself and then re-collected myself from this rock.

If you believe in divine timing, which I do, it becomes incredible to imagine that timing and predestined connections span through and between lifetimes. The puzzle is complex and multidimensional and just became a lot more interesting for me.

It sounds crazy and yet, it doesn't. If you only live once, then go for it! Do the crazy thing with abandon. Write the truth. Paint from your soul. Cry with the rock. See what happens. If, on the other hand, you live a thousand times, then go for it BIG. Take the risk! What have you possibly got to lose?

DISCOMFORT SERVES A PURPOSE

I am so uncomfortable right now. The mess is huge in my house. Every corner, every surface reflects a big project back to me. The garage is so full it is practically oozing stuff. The back yard, my space, is littered with hen poop, dog poop and way too many cats. I have ideas I am aching to act on, but the laundry list of things to do before the creativity can begin is soooo long. It makes me tired, exhausted actually, to think of all that I need to do.

Sometimes I wish I could be a cat, my only requirement for the day to log my twenty hours of sleep, the only hard choice - to sleep under the covers of the bed or curled up on a big chair amongst the pillows? My husband walks in, looks at me and thinks, "She's at her computer again." Little does he know.

The work of telling, revealing, mirroring and uncovering seems to be my destiny, the cost of what is to be here, now. Oh, I forgot to mention the piles of bills, papers, essential and urgently important PTA stuff that needs to be addressed last week. It is all piled like layers of mica rock, slippery and unstable, ready to slide off my desk. I am now taking this moment to write to you and to myself this reminder of the bigger picture.

This is all temporary. The discomfort, the mess, the hen poop and the cats are but a flash in time, insignificant details to pepper my life this morning with the seasoning required to establish a culinary contrast. These are the acrid spices of my dish alone. They are but the palate cleanser for the fun, deliciously satisfying main course that will be served when I have cleared my plate...and my garage.

NOT QUITE WHAT YOU HAD IN MIND

I suspect that fierce self-criticism is universal. We see ourselves one way and are shocked when we glimpse a photograph of ourselves and see someone different, literally, not quite what we had in mind.

I was taking pictures of my mother this afternoon. My mother is nearly 61 years of age but very beautifully seasoned. She has taken very good care of herself, exercising regularly, wearing sunscreen, imbibing on nothing stronger than coffee and maintaining an impeccable sense of style.

I am always surprised when I take her picture and experience the reaction that I did today of, "I look like a snail with a bowl on my head". This opinion is never what I am thinking when looking through the lens. It just surprises me that a woman as confident, accomplished and beautiful as my mother can think this of herself. Of course, her sense of humor is strong and part of her beauty is her ability to laugh at herself, but I still don't see it. She didn't look like a snail with a bowl on her head, a remark commenting on her new feng shui hair cut; she looked like Mom, the beautiful.

I realize that I, too, have had moments when observing a photograph of myself that I felt viscerally that the picture in question did not reflect the real me. But let's face it, who hasn't felt that way? Pictures are beautiful because they capture a moment. They freeze time. I don't usually throw pictures away for this very reason. They are all good, even when they are bad.

MEMOIRS OF A WICKED STEPMOTHER

I really do try not to be wicked, but sometimes, it seems to be inevitable. I have been a stepmother for almost ten years, surviving the teen years of one daughter, now in college, and existing as the wicked one to another in high school.

The oldest, now nineteen, was my sparring partner from very early on. I have never been much of a fighter but this curly haired fireball seemed to always bring a fight out of me. We have had some really good ones, screaming, crying, the inevitable ripple effect of the *real* parents catching on to the brawl and the predictable apology. Always the apology. I am really good at *that* part. I am always willing to say, "I'm sorry" and acknowledge my hurtful actions. Maybe this is the way I have lasted so long in this role.

I realized this past Thanksgiving what the gift of this relationship is. I am by nature, passive most of the time. I am reasonable and neutral and can take criticism without lashing out. I am good at *not* fighting. The only person with whom I have fought with on a somewhat regular basis is my beloved stepdaughter.

You might now be thinking, **what a wicked witch - fighting with a child**! I would tend to agree with you. The gift is that this truth has been so revealed. Fighting is human and since childhood, I haven't done enough of it. Now that I am aware of this, I am secretly hoping that the urge to argue will subside and instead, I will be supplanted with a knowing smile and a silent giggle. Now that I know this about myself, there is no reason to continue with this low level of human behavior. Besides, my partner is intelligent and gaining confidence and it just makes me look bad.

I may be wicked, yes, but at least I am honest and as I've mentioned before, I am imperfect, but fully human.

THE BEST GIFTS

The best gifts are the ones that create a visceral memory. My favorite gifts of past Christmases were the ones that gave me a happy moment to cherish.

Every year, my kids, husband and I return to the Santa Barbara Mission on Christmas Eve. We don't go for the Christmas Eve Catholic Mass, although the kids do like to stick their heads in the door to smell the incense and listen to the music.

We return every year to be together, under the stars, to gaze thoughtfully at the life sized Nativity scene. We giggle about the clothes the three kings are dressed in, commenting on the lack of an arm on one of them. Tom reminds the kids what the tree kings' names were. We like to hear our small children say 'Balthazar', 'Malchior' and 'Casper'. We talk about the story of the birth of Jesus and why he was a great person. It is not a Christian discussion, but more of a human discussion- one that leaves me wanting to be a better person.

The kids always play tag in the dark and we are almost always blessed with the sound of the Mission bells, which is one of our favorite gifts on Christmas Eve. Finally, every year, we take family pictures in front of the Nativity scene. My first year, when Tom and I were just dating, the picture is of me, him, his two daughters and their baby sister, Faith. Now the family shots get re-mixed and sometimes we group into eye color, like the blue eyed people and get a picture of the Mothers (me and my step daughters' mom, and the three kids with blue eyes).

We always conduct this ritual as a big family, so that every child has the loving presence of both parents present. It is these moments that I cherish. Every year this tradition serves as a reminder

100

that our family is special because we choose to work together and love each other, as best we can. My hope is for you to have these types of moments that sear your memory with the joys of family and the true meaning of Christmas.

DESTINY

If you are here, you are meant to feel pain. You are meant to feel sorrow and create sorrow for another. If you are here, you are meant to fall apart. You are destined to have calamities in which all you have striven for dissipates into nothingness.

If you are here, you are meant to struggle in relationships. You will let the people you love down and be let down by people you love.

If you are here, you are meant to judge and be judged. You will set your karma by judging another in what you describe as a wrongful action. You will live to experience a situation just as wrongful so that you gain compassion for yourself and others.

If you are here, you will feel want and need. You will feel the bitter chill of winter and not be able to warm yourself. If you are here, you will feel hunger and thirst, filth and disease. You will feel the pain of your body, in a state of illness and attempt the lonely struggle back to health.

If you are here, you will feel mediocre, and second-guess your best ideas and achievements. You will feel alone in a household full of people who know you.

If you are here, you will feel the anguish and powerlessness that come from witnessing the wrongs that people create; starvation, devastation, consumption, pollution, rape, homelessness, war, politics, suburban sprawl, extinction.

If you are here, you will feel the pain of these things on many levels. You will feel the anguish of the loss of someone you have loved more deeply than you ever thought possible.

If you are here, you are surviving these things.

If you are here, you have hope or the possibility of having hope.

You have seen sunsets and sunrises that bring tears to your eyes. If you are here, you have tasted food that allowed you to imagine heaven. If you are here, you have had your thirst quenched and achieved a state of warmth that provides you comfort. You have seen the beauty in a flower. You have marveled at the joyous behavior of children.

If you are here, you have been loved and possibly, you have loved.

If you are here, you have laughed. You have had the opportunity to say, "I'm sorry." You may have suffered through devastation of untold magnitude, but you still have the ability to find joy.
You may have lost everything, but found that as you live, you have the ability to find good in your situation. You may even have a sense of humor. You may find the comedy in your tragedy.

If you are here, on Earth, these things are true.

If not for pain, how could we appreciate contentment? If not for cold, how could we savor warmth? If not for loss, how could we appreciate all that we have, when we have it? If not for compassion, how could we find ourselves free of judgment? If not for destruction, how could we create? If not for despair, how could we measure joy?

This place and time are not meant to be easy for us, but designed to be a place of challenge and difficulty. How better can we learn but in this way?

If you feel uncertain at times, questioning your divine purpose, you are right on schedule. Have you ever stopped and thought, could this be my divine purpose, just breathing in and out with my senses ready to take it all in?

Could it be possible that learning to be human, flawed, destined for mistakes and lovable anyway is the only real destiny? Any other worldly impact only being part of each individual's experience? Is it possible that the greatest achievement is to live in love when things fall apart around you? Loving yourself through mistakes and mishaps. Loving others by making amends when you have done the hurting. Loving yourself and others by forgiving them for wrongs against you and reserving judgment for the actions of others.

Could the greatest purpose be to love the gifts that you encounter on any given day and having the insight to see all situations from a higher perspective?

If you are here, as long as you are here, these things will be yours. They are mine and I wouldn't rush out just yet.
When it is over, when you are gone, when it is all just a memory, there's no way to return, except in that ghostly form of a memory. It may not seem as "bad" from a distance. It may seem precious though. I have a feeling it will, and that this moment must be savored, this accomplishment of breathing in and out honored. I am doing it. Living my destiny.

CHANGED

I have metamorphosed into another person. Not someone thinner with different hair and lipstick, I'm actually different: changed. I suspected that it was happening. I explained the tremors, the rapid heartbeat away as a vibrational shift. But I felt bad. Really really bad. Now, from the other end, I know I have shifted. I have let go. I have changed. It's a good change.

I vibrate now, kind of a buzz, when I am barely awake in the predawn morning. I see myself bathed in blue light and I wonder how people would react to me if they saw me shopping at Trader Joe's, scolding my four year old, glowing in ethereal blue. I wonder, and I know.

That's the thing, it seems with the change, with the shift has come the peace of knowing and not needing to know at the same time. I can go into my body and address any ailments, then I can travel out and see you, glowing green from your heart, healing right before my closed, dark-entrenched eyes.

It's fun, this movement through space. It helps to know geography and the cellular landscape of a human body, just because it is more exciting to be direct in your actions. I keep getting a little tinge of surprise when the crystal orbs I am holding start to radiate in my palms when meditating, as if I am validated that they have energy. I am surprised. I am not surprised.

It is fun, this adventure. It is fun to have these abilities and tools at my disposal. I am having fun in my new body with my new mind metamorphosed from caterpillar into butterfly.

IN THE AIR

I've been waking up early. Wide awake at three, four A.M. It's not insomnia, because, I feel rested, and what wakes me up is fun. I begin to vibrate. It's like an alarm clock inside my body on silent mode.

Today, I could feel my lips being tickled as the vibration was taking place. It's not a seizure, mind you. I know what a cerebral seizure feels like.

I had three unexplained seizures, without medically known origin, when I was ten. In the ten-year-old type of seizure, the body shakes violently. The air is forced in and out of the lungs in a violent, sucking hyperventilation. The consciousness is alert to the mayhem, embarrassed by the sucking sounds, perplexed by the fish-out-of-water flipping about, and finally, rather fascinated by the sounds that emerge from the flaccid, drooling lips, when what is clearly being said is "I'm FINE. Do not call 9I I!" But what the ear and stunned onlooker hears is "THHUUU SSSSSUUUUH UUUOOUUUU" Imagine Boris Karloff's Frankenstein. Yep. That's it. So, having experienced a real seizure, I know that this three AM vibration is not one.

So, it's early. It's still. My body is doing its fun little buzz that takes my consciousness to some very cool places. You should see the flips and happy spirals energy can do at this time of the morning. Imagine a very happy dolphin, flipping around in and out of the water. It's almost like that, but more poetic, faster, more multi-dimensional and with prettier colors. If you are feeling a twinge of jealousy right now, I've got news. I think this is the way of things to come. Call it an inkling. Don't close your mind off to the possibility thinking, "that'll never be me", because I am willing to put money down to the contrary.

Soon, in fact very soon, you too will have to consciously ground your joy, and I don't mean with a mortar and pestle. I mean, send it down the cord. Mellow it out. We can't really go through our day doing psychic flips and spirals while driving on the rainy highway to Costco, now can we?

I am almost forty. Forty year old women who are PTA Presidents, have to be able to cool their elation when need be. Tempering it and then tucking it neatly under their raincoats so as not to upset their friends.

My advice to you is just keep breathing through each day, you're doing fine, you're right on track, you don't have to do anything special, just notice when it comes and just keep breathing in out in out. Yes, like that.

METAPHOR

Today I watched STAR WARS, Episode III, Revenge of the Sith, on the couch with the little DVD player my kids use on long trips to pass the time. I drank my coffee, allowed my son, Aidan to join me, watching together the poetic progression of Anakin Skywalker, the chosen one, the one pre-destined to restore order to The Galaxy, evolve into Darth Vader, apprentice to the misinformed leader of the Sith, Supreme Chancellor Palpatine, soon to be cloaked and hooded Emperor with some serious wrinkle problems.

While watching this I kept thinking how brilliant the body of work is as a whole. It serves as a metaphoric model of our own society, human history and future, in such a beautifully stylish way.

I have always identified with the Force as "God", or that energy most of us now refer to as "The Universe". My childhood (and adulthood, for that matter) was ruled by this concept I recognized as truth.

There is an energy that binds all things. This energy can be harnessed for strength, for information, for a clear view that sight could never provide. The force is about feelings. "Check your feelings, Luke". Third chakra, baby! It's all about feelings. Gut feelings never lie, because it's The Force guiding you.

So, getting back to my day... I was loving this movie. I had only seen it once, in the theater, when it came out a few years ago. I really enjoyed it then, but thought the acting was weak, the special effects too numerous and the story too complicated to follow. It just shows where I was and am in my evolution, because today, all I could keep saying to myself is, *This is mastery. This is genius. This is perfect. This is speaking to my heart truths upon truths. This is George Lucas's gift to the human race.* This may be how the

110

human race, how all those younglings, learn the ways of The Force soon enough that they survive and thrive in this vibrational transition.

Aidan, who is almost five years old, followed this film and agreed with me on every point I shared with him, right down to the totally cool T-Bird-esque ship Obi Wan takes to track down General Grievous on a planet in the Outer Rim. He said, "cool ship" while I silently thought "cool ship".

FAMILY DISCOUNT

Walk into any bookstore and you will find a dozen best sellers that advise you to ask for what you want and need, actually feel what it's like to have that which you desire, with the implication that only then can the universe provide.

So many souls won't even ask. They shut the door on themselves, actually rarely even opening it in the first place, before they risk having the door slammed on their needy, wanting hearts. What a waste. Thankfully, I have become rather good at the asking, and then letting go of the result that may or may not manifest itself. My track record is sound. This technique works. You need proof? No problem.

I received my first wish box when I was a teenager in the 1980's. I remember that it was a gift and that it was wooden and simple and somewhat mystically painted with copper swirls or triangles or something. The wish box came with simple instructions. Place your written wishes in the box. I remember writing my "wishes". You know, all those things that would lighten the burden of worry from my heart, on tiny strips of paper.

I usually wrote the requests as polite inquiries, that I may please have.... oh let's say as an example... a means to go to college, always followed by a sincere *thank you* just for taking the time to consider the request. Two years later, from this inquiry, I somehow found myself in line to take the picture for my student I.D. at California State University, Long Beach. My sister Stacy, who played volleyball there on a full scholarship, had brought me home an application and henpecked me until I mailed it, and my transcripts in.

The wish box received new wishes varying in magnitude of levels of probability that they would happen, sometimes desperately begging,"Please let Andrew marry me!" Somehow I never gave up on the box, even when some of the really really important events, like Andrew marrying me, just refused to take place. Oh, but then, I have patience. I never took the long wait as a no answer. I just figured the wish was fulfilled somewhere in the future. Me and Andrew, simple gold bands in a courthouse, with no beautiful dress and no bride's maids - I didn't need all that- Oh, just to be Mrs. Pott. I chuckle now, from this vantage point, at this sweet girl who refuses to give up on things that obviously aren't for her. Ahhh, youth.

     When the wishes were fulfilled, like graduating from college, the strip of paper would be thrown away to make room for new wishes. Sometimes I would clean out old wishes, not wanting them any more. Either way, I was always relieved of the burden of worry that my life would unfold in ways I could not foresee. Like a present. My wish-making track record includes the receipt of:

A real job with a salary, as opposed to a paycheck.

A cool apartment in Santa Barbara with a shoe box-sized ocean view when you looked from the level of the kitchen counter with your cheek pressed up against the glass,

Dates,

Boyfriends,

Friends,

A husband/family,

A baby,

A house, we could afford, - actually the house we wanted but were told we absolutely could not buy because it wasn't nor would it ever be for sale,

My dream car,

My destiny/soul's purpose, made clear to me,

My soul mate, (who happens to be the man I married nearly ten years ago),

Here's what the wish box/Universe has denied me:

My career in pharmaceutical sales,

My career as a therapeutic gemstone jewelry practitioner,

My career as creator of uplifting spiritual enlightment-inducing cards,

My perpetually flat stomach,

My freedom in the form of bringing in my own income/ AKA, my "financial" independence.

As a side note, I have defied the universe on this one, because I have still acted as if the money was mine, making all the hard choices, like "should I spend $133 dollars on something so frivolous as a fully reversible emerald and purple, full length cape, just because I really want it, even though I run out of money each month before the next paycheck comes in for managing the household's expenses?" Yep. I bought it.

I'm telling you, I have gotten pretty gutsy in the requests I've been making to the universe these days. In the past two months I have ordered a pay-off of all outstanding mortgages, a pay off of my car, various home improvements, money to travel, and then some.

I called up Stacy, my sister, and left a message on the family answering machine saying, and I quote, "Hi, this is Shelley and I'd like to place an order from the Universe for equipment to film the feature length, major release documentary I am going to make. I would also like to order a computer large enough to edit this masterpiece with the highest quality. In addition, the time and finances required to make this endeavor come to fruition. And put a rush on it, Universe, this project needs to start yesterday."

When the Universe Rep. called me back, I had her read me my order, just to make sure she got it right. She assured me with confidence that it was on its way. I have to say, it is so nice dealing with people you can trust. It just alleviates the need to worry about things like, *did she get the size and quantity right? Does she know that I need resources of all types to make this happen, not just the money? Is she aware that I need a support staff, like an agent and an editor, and a secretary and someone to carry my film equipment through airport terminals so that I may leave my hands free for holding on to those of my children and husband?*

Oh, this Rep is good. She really gets the nuances of the unspoken request. She just takes the liberty of inflating your order to include the things you didn't know you needed. I am so pleased with her service that I have sent a business reply card to the Universe, thanking them for sending Stacy to me as my Rep. I am sure a raise is in store for her. I think she's already ordered it. Oh, and she is so good, I didn't even need to pull that old, overly used card, requesting the "family discount".

WHAT'S THE WORST THAT COULD HAPPEN?

My mother used to ask me this question when I would be fretful with worry over something. When I was seven, this seemed to be a constant condition for me. We had moved many times by the time I was seven.

We moved again, sometime after the school year had already started. I had grown fond of Mrs. Bennett, my second grade teacher at La Marina. I had survived the wetting-my-pants-on-a-rainy-day incident, the fire on the field where nobody did what we had learned in the fire drills. I even went unscathed upon witnessing one of my older sisters on her way to the office with a big dollop of bird poop on her shoulder. And just like that, all that I had been through seemed like a day at the Fair compared to the way I felt at Pacific School on my first day, mid year.

I was thrust into a classroom with kids I didn't know, forced to sit in the front, at a table instead of at a desk with the other kids, and told to copy the spelling words off a chart in the front of the room, by my new teacher, Mrs. Yaz.

Ohhhh, my stomach instinctually curls up into a nervous ball at the thought of that fateful day. Mrs. Yaz was cold, hard, very old and from my adult perspective, way way past the prime age of retirement. The woman was actually a hazard to the children she was hired to teach and care for during their very formative years.

I have come to see the age of seven as the magic age. The age when we become ourselves. We are all pretty much the same person we were at seven; with more experience more self control and perhaps a more worldly view of things. I was sensitive, quiet, introspective, secretly very funny, tall for my age, had a spark of confidence that would later ignite into the fire that now burns brightly within me.

116

Oh, but I digress. Back to second grade. The first thing I did on that day was copy the wrong spelling words.

My memory has edited much of the year from my grasp. I can tell you that I spent a lot of time in the school nurse's office with a tummy ache (yeah- my third chakra- gut feeling was telling me to do what ever I needed to do to keep away from Mrs. Yaz!); I stayed home a lot with "illness". I even remember meeting with the school principal on a couple of occasions to discuss any "problems" I was having. Pretty simply, the only problem I had was that sticky black energy in front of the classroom that was trying her best to extinguish any light she saw.

That year, I read lots of picture books with one foot crossed over my bent knee, lying on the nurse's table. It was fine when I took care of myself. It was painful when I was forced to bear witness to Mrs. Yaz's contained cruelty. I saw how she treated a boy who fell back in his chair (yes he was tipping it- he was a boy though, not doing anything abnormal or unexpected for such a gender) who had a smear of blood on his hand as it passed through his hair at the impact sight, I ached inside with grief. She would not even permit him to go to the nurse's office. I had probably used up all the nurses passes by then.

The best thing that happened in second grade was meeting my friend Lara. Lara and I talk almost every day. Yesterday, I was talking to Lara about one of the concepts that has recently come to me in my new vibrational state of bliss.

The idea is this: As long as you have your consciousness, you are free. You are free to exist in joy or pain, you are free to vibrate in love of be eaten alive by fear and sorrow. You are free from the bondage of everyone else's will but your own.

Even if you are wrongfully imprisoned in Guantanamo Bay in a concrete isolation chamber with no light, you are free. Even if you are imprisoned in a body that has been paralyzed from the nose down, you are free. Even if you have killed five hundred thousand

117

innocent people because you were ordered to do so by your commanding officer, you are free. You have your consciousness, you have free will, you are free.

Imagine a world filled with people who grasp this concept. There would be an easement of pain, there would be a lifting of suffering, there would be an erasure of remorse, of self sabotage, of guilt, of revenge, of a need to attack before being attacked, a need to victimize before becoming a victim. There would be no victims. There would be no inflictors of pain. There would be only choice and free individuals who choose to put their weapons down, forgive themselves for atrocities/mistakes they have made and make amends to those they have harmed. There would be forgiveness, and motion in a forward direction.

Imagine this concept in every situation where there is strife, struggle and pain. Imagine the difference it would make if you could never be a victim. If the threat of "rape" were no longer the worst thing that could happen to you. If death were not the worst thing that could happen to you. If loss, or a broken heart, or being wrong were not the worst things that could happen to you.

A NEW SET OF BOOBS

I met a woman at a party recently. Her name is Jill. Jill, and I were sipping wine, gobbling gourmet pizza and talking trash when I asked her, "What are your plans for Valentine's Day?" She said that she wanted to do something really hot for her husband of eighteen years. I started to offer up suggestions.

-"Get rid of the kids" - There were three- "Check!" she said.

- "Turn off all electric things, except perhaps music, and light the house with candles." - "oooh good! Keep going!" she said.

-"When he comes home, answer the door in sexy lingerie, or a slinky robe". This is where the conversation got interesting.

"I think I'll wear nothing but tassels on my nipples." she said, "these boobs are for him!"

"Oh, are they new?" I inquired.

"Yes." Jill said calmly, " I had breast cancer, these are new. I got them in December."

Then Jill went on to tell me her breast cancer story. She said she got the diagnosis in September. That her old breasts were so flat, and saggy that the mammography technician didn't even have to spread them out to have a good scan of them. "My kids sucked the life out of them. They nursed me to death!" Good, I thought, they served their purpose.

"When I found out I had breast cancer, I had a Bye Bye Boobies Party. We served Margaritas and had m&ms made that said 'ta ta ta-tas'. I got rip roaring drunk with my friends and sent my breasts off with flair!...

"I fell in love with my husband during my cancer", Jill added, "We have been married eighteen years and he took two months off from work to do my job for me while I was recovering. One month in September and another full month in December.

"He did all the cooking, shopping, picking up and dropping off of the three kids, all that I do, he took over, showing me how much he respected me in my job as wife and mother."

I hugged Jill and thanked her for bravely being who she was and for sharing with me, a "stranger", such beautiful intimacy.

I saw it. The beauty in the tragedy. The joy in the pain. The *perfect* imperfection.

NOTHING IS EVER LOST

The Law of Conservation of Energy generally states that nothing is ever lost. In a chemical reaction or in a physical action, the same amount of energy that goes in comes out, shifted and altered, changed, but still there. As humans we have been making sense of this phenomenon for hundreds or even thousands of years.

If you have a camera, especially a digital one, you may have noticed an infrequent orb of light in a picture. These orbs have become so frequent in my photographs that I have gone way beyond simply noticing them and moved into the realm of experimentation. I have asked them to appear and they have. Asked them to leave with the same result. Noticed their numbers and their intensity increase when there are lots of kids around, on Halloween, at Christmastime, at places like the Santa Barbara Mission and have made a note of how dusty a room may have been prior to taking an orb-filled photo.

I suspect the orbs represent energies. Possibly they are the energies that represent souls that are not contained in a body. It is hard to verify these statements, so all are supposition at this point. But the point is, that all around you, every day there are energies. They are inhibited in their ability to communicate. We are inhibited by our inability to see and or acknowledge them. Although we exist side by side.

I have told my kids that they should never be afraid of ghosts because someday they may be one. I say, "how would you feel if you were just there, wanting to play but your playmate could not see you, or hear you, and if you could get them to see or hear you, they run away screaming? How frustrated would you be? " Just imagine yourself on the other side of the conservation of energy equation and gather some empathy for your friends who are already there. They are not gone, they are simply changed.

BE AN AMATEUR

It takes a lot of guts to be perfectly OK looking foolish. I think this as I am bumping along from long term parking to the Alaska Airlines gate with camera bag and tripod slung across each shoulder, laptop case and wheeled bag in tow. I am redefining myself at thirty nine. I am a documentarian and cinematographer, author and artist. I need new business cards.

I think about this as I sit at the gate. This willingness to not know what I am doing until I know what I'm doing. I contemplate this comfort I feel in being an amateur until I can show my abilities as a seasoned and reliable professional.

Every great artist begins as an amateur. Every musician starts with a faulty note. Every expert originates at a question she must answer for herself, a path she must walk alone, an experience she is destined to savor from rough beginning to satisfied end.

At thirty nine, I begin my first shoot outside Santa Barbara of potentially new people who don't know me as anything but what I say I am, a documentarian, cinematographer and author. In the airport in Seattle, I decide to make my own business cards out of card stock. On the cards I put Terra Celeste Productions on the front and my name on the back with my new title and contact information.

While in Alaska, I shoot many hours of tape, learning that when I leave the camera unattended, I like the subjects to be higher in the frame. I learn that the shot looks better, feels more authentic if I stay out of the scene and do not talk, which is hard for me, as I can be chatty. I learn that I like shooting at a slower speed, like a movie camera, because the footage feels warmer, easier to connect with as opposed to the clinical, cold, more real speed of a video camera.

I capture beautiful shots. I capture absolute magic. I witness souls being revealed.

I am learning. I am a little less of an amateur, just by doing. The film project I am making is about people striving to live their truth, seeking their bliss, being brave enough to just *do it*. It has occurred to me that this is exactly what I am doing. I see myself returning for more shots in Alaska with people I have met who are willing to be amateurs while they seek their bliss, live their truth and become experts in the field of their own happiness.

LIGHTEN YOUR HEART

Give up anger.

Give up blaming yourself and or others.

Give up stress- you will not be "late"- it's divine timing.

Give up resentment- 'if he had done this, I would be happy now'.

Give up resentment- 'If I had left sooner, we wouldn't be late'.

Give up fear- fear of losing, fear of being wrong, fear of winning, fear of making mistakes, fear.

Of everything.

Give up remorse-there are no mistakes. If it was said, it needed to be said. Say you are sorry if you have hurt someone's feelings.

Give up embarrassment- stop caring that people are looking at you. Just be you, who ever that may be.

Give up humility- stop trying to keep yourself bagged up- just be.

Making amends frees you, even if you were not wrong, even if it was an accident, even if you didn't mean to, even if you did nothing, even if it was totally on purpose and you meant every word you said, making amends frees you.

Globally, people who have suffered genocide, rape, imprisonment, the horrors of our current world, will tell you, that when they have received amends for the wrongs done against them, and they have accepted the amends and forgiven, the heart heals, and they can move on. Life goes on. The worst thing that can happen to you can be amended. The worst thing that can happen to you is not the worst thing that can happen to you. Get it?

Ask your guides/angels for assistance and divine timing. This way you will know that everything that happens during your day is perfect and you won't need to fret, struggle or get cranky when, from your perspective, things aren't going right.

Expect to have fun and you will.

Say please and thank you to your guides and angels.

Leave all your fear, scowls, worries, resentment, blame, etc. in the big dumpster at home.

Remember, if you said it, it needed to be said, if you did it, it needed to be done, and you are never a victim, only a student. Learn the lesson and get on with your day.

If you want it, ask for it.

If you want to do it, do it.

If you want to say it, say it.

If you want it to happen, make it happen.

Don't look back. Start now.

Now is the perfect time.

Remain light-hearted in the seeking of your inevitable enlightenment.

the end.

MORE

My personal goal has always been to nurture and encourage people to be themselves and to live fully. I do this by acting as an example a lot. I do that scary thing, that risky thing and say, *see? It's not so hard! Come on, you can do it too! I'll show you how!* I think anyone who really knows me would agree that this is true.

My professional goals have been driven by my desire to help people. I have been pretty creative about how I have been able to affect people positively from the location of the chair in my office. For many years, it was by creating therapeutic gemstone jewelry, that would hopefully, when worn, encourage growth, nurturing, expansion and the blossoming of each individual I created a piece for.

I also wrote a blog, associated with my jewelry website so that people could have access to my words of encouragement. From that blog, through much editing, came this book.

I am now working on a documentary film project that I hope will inspire a spark of change in each person who sees it. My goal for this book and for the film project is to show how other people, including myself, are striving every day to see the magic and the potential for bliss that each moment holds.

The idea of happiness, success and living a blissful state, is different for each individual, so my documentary film project will capture all types of people in different stages of pursuit of their truth, and this happy state of being.

I will do whatever it takes to be of service in this way of encouragement and nurturing. However I can, I would like to encourage you to be yourself, unearth your dreams, strive to make them real and live your bliss, all the while keeping in mind that you don't have to do any of it perfectly. You just have to do it.